Y0-DFA-807

Tillable Soil

Poems by
Heidi Nightengale

Tillable Soil $10.00
Poems by **Heidi Nightengale**
Clare Songbirds Publishing House Chapbook Series
ISBN 978-1-947653-01-6
Clare Songbirds Publishing House
Tillable Soil © 2107 Heidi Nightengale
All Rights Reserved. Clare Songbirds Publishing House retains right to reprint.
Permission to reprint individual poems must be obtained from the author who owns the copyright.

Printed in the United States of America
SECOND EDITION

Clare Songbirds Publishing House Mission Statement:
Clare Songbirds Publishing House was established to provide a print forum for the creation of limited edition, fine art from poets and writers, both established and emerging. We strive to reignite and continue a tradition of quality, accessible literary arts to the national and international community of writers, and readers. We support our literary artists with high quality services and on-going support. Chapbook manuscripts and art quality poetry broadsides are carefully chosen for their ability to propel the expansion of art and ideas in literary form. We provide an accessible way to promote the art of words in order to resonate with, and impact, readers not yet familiar with the siren song of poets and writers. Clare Songbirds Publishing House espouses a singular cultural development where poetry creates community and becomes commonplace in public places.

Clare Songbirds Publishing House
140 Cottage Street
Auburn, New York 13021
www.ClareSongbirdspub.com

Contents

Finding a Copy of Out of Africa (published 1938)	7
Pale Blue Dot	8
Recalculating	9
Why I cannot spell Rhyme	10
Special Valentine's Offer	11
If I could be a tomato	12
Archipelago	13
Fourth Grade Autobiography: 1969	14
Season of Decay	18
Winter's Valentine	20
Weeping and Laughing	21
The Night Aunt Goldie Died	22
When the Creaking Started	23
Things Left Behind	24
Sunflowers At Highway Speed	26
Looking for My Mother	27
The Daughter of a Tenant Farmer's Son	28
Tillable Soil	30

Publication credits for poems appearing in *Tillable Soil*

"Finding a Copy of Out of Africa (published 1938)" *The Healing Muse,* V.11, N.1

"Winter's Valentine," *aaduna, Four for the Fourth,* 2017

*For the natural world
which taught me to live
among poetry*

March 2018

For Willow~

Your Name itself is one which inspires poetry & the beauty of the natural world!

♡— Heidi

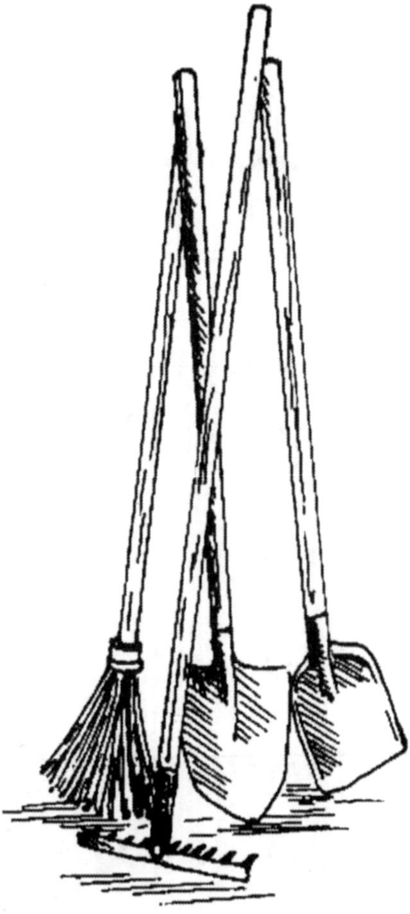

Finding a Copy of Out of Africa
(published 1938)

I felt at the sight of it, like understanding
the mysterious mindfulness of church, and
stayed a long time alone before bringing
down the news. I rested like the trunk
among the piles of black walnuts
fallen through the roof of the barn.

He has pushed himself through the gene carrying
memory to leave a granddaughter,
firstborn of firstborn daughters,
the first edition to replace the paperback
that had served me as a saving place for dreams
of my own farm one day—
a farm for wildflower seeds mixed among the coffee.

And *yes* I thought; Africa had remembered him,
who had left the book packed in a trunk for me to find
when I was twice the age he ever got to be.

Pale Blue Dot

In a moment of scientific serendipity,
Carl Sagan called for Voyager 1 to turn around
just as it speeded out of our solar system.
"Turn around. Turn the camera to take
one last picture of earth as we leave for beyond."
And the photo was taken. In that deepest
recess of space. The photo posted back our
earth: a pale blue dot, smaller than the
red-blue blood of a pin prick on a finger tip
back here on earth where we were voyaging
to grocery stores, work in warehouses, painters' steps
upon ladders,
children in blue pools of water where young eyelashes
gleamed with drops of glittered water,
ants carried bread and pieces of cheese curl.
So small it seems to matter not that men in prison
murdered, or a mother lied to a crying child.
Small and pale as a lover's eyes:
sometimes deep blue and sometimes spattered as if
in 0.12 pixels of pale blue dots.

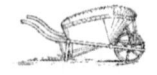

Recalculating

Anthony Weiner stole my poem.
He said, "I have worn
out the recalculating message that we hear
on the GPS." His metaphor was about
forgiveness, he says. But his words
linger, malinger as I travel along alone.

I think, when driving and take a wrong turn
and hear "recalculating, recalculating," I know
that I *must* keep going in this new direction—can't turn back.
Yes, Instead I take the dirt road and turn off the GPS.

I make my own mid-course correction
and view a family on the steps of their trailer
filled with flood waters twice in the last year.
I stop and smell the wafting of a pot of coffee from their
rotting trailer. They are my a-political, poor
experts in fleshy recalculations who offer me coffee—
"The pot's always on," they tell me.

They tell me, too, that the farmer
who owns the wilting fields
around them, would be pleased to have me stop
and pluck the blueberries still left in his hedgerow,
pick a few sunflowers and dig up some day
lilies, they offer me as I share with them that
I have always wanted to plant wild lilies along
my garden shed in my tidy lawn
far upstate from this dirt road. in the privacy
of this mountain foot hill; a humble, clean place of
my recalculation.

Why I cannot spell Rhyme

I can never remember if the *h* comes first,
or is it the *y?* But I do remember that
with mine, rhyme is deep and half,
internal and between
the words and not often the end of a line.
It is the same with the small black-red cherries
that appear as sentimental tear drops in August
on the weeping cherry tree;
the kind of cherries that only the birds
can eat and know, taking them inside
somewhere deep, maybe half filling themselves
with each piece of the tree's tiny fruit
pushed through the hidden ringed lines
of the weeping tree's ragged trunk
waiting for each small and grateful beak.

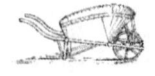

Special Valentine's Offer

is spelled in red neon letters
above the child waiting with me
for the bus. Her hands are blue black
in the breath curling cold
and her shoulders ground
to cremains with the bulk of a backpack.

We sit alone together.
She smells of rice, beans, cooking oil.
I do not know my smell.
I dare to ask the child.

"Like a pillow stitched with lavender
secretly pocketed within," she whirs.
I startle with warmth at her vocabulary
and metaphor:
Not one of rice, beans and cooking oil.

And the warmth spreads to reddening
shame, the toxin flushing my face,
the face of an old woman once a girl
with a shared tooth brush,
tight shoes, the fragrance of steamed cabbage
and her uncle's cigarettes clinging to her hair;
a girl who left notes cut
in heart shapes, prolific peace offerings
on her mother's pillow,
after raging over homemade valentines
when she really wanted to give the
boxed ones in the store.

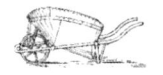

If I could be a tomato

for Marin and Jack

I would be the orange almost red one
plump like a fifty-five-year old woman
from summer sweetened rains,
and the stuff they call miracle grow,
or ice cream and Raisinets-- in my case.
I would be dripping lightly with morning dew,
and later dropping droplets from a child's afternoon
watering can which slicks my skin for purposeful
lack of umbrella like the dizzy with craze substitute teacher
who dances in summer rains.

And I would wait to be
picked like the happy fat sun burnt aunt
chosen by a favorite niece, a one-of-kind nephew
who bite me open
standing bare foot in the garden
while I drool kisses of sun-warmed,
succulent summer memories and magic
down their fragrant chins.

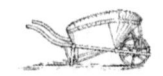

Archipelago

Kathleen, we are bound by two a.m. talks; once
over the smell of coffee, now on either side of phone lines.
We find entertainment in memories of Oliver's refrigerator
always humming with emptiness but for his light beer cans
and popsicles in the freezer. You tell me the story
of two pregnant women; one birthing a bright boy,
the other born still.

We never move to smooth the hard point;
Sitting hours sifting like bugs though old flour.
We speak the difference of your mother
who does not know the smell of marijuana
and mine who could throw a curse on a Sunday
that flowed like wind in a wheat field.
You are light and I am serious:
Always trying to get at vital business, and ready
to make plans for the walk of words
that will bridge another evening's talk.

Fourth Grade Autobiography: 1969

I.

We turned our papers up front, paper over head, paper over head in automation. The kid with his name on an owl that read, "teacher's assistant" on the daily job board scurried to the front to collect them into a happy jumble of something that I felt would be important in the end. I didn't feel that way about all my assignments. Next day, our papers were passed back carefully by Mrs. Stinson--not the classroom owl assistant from the job board. She walked each aisle and placed our papers writing side down. "Students, you all have more work to do. Turn over your papers, read my notes and begin again."

II.

Mrs. Stinson's notes: (in red): *Good first draft. Revise. Revise?* I was delighted to know I could *revise* my autobiography! I started with a force that broke pencil tips immediately. I did not wet my bed. I did not hate the red felt coat with white piping that looked like a church coat, not a school coat. I did not steal cherry life savers when I was five while my mother was busy with the checkout lady at the Red and White Market. In fact, I *had* to revise that because I felt so bad about those lifesavers that I snuck them into the outside trash burning barrel which only my father was allowed to go near. I had not tasted one. I had not even opened them. And I fought a feeling for years waiting to learn the word for what the feeling was that crawled up without a call to curl and tease its way into my stomach and mind leaving me hungerless. But I *did* leave in the part about my drawings of the witch from the "Fractured Fairy Tales." I could draw her plump, triangular body, little trunk legs, and perfectly pointed hat (which I asked for on every Christmas list). I was sure my drawings of her looked just like she did on morning TV while I watched –one eye on TV the other on the window for the bus. I drew her on walls, my brother's desk, the back of my school work papers, my mother's freshly painted walls. I revised the part about drawing her in a library book, though. That might save some inquiries. I kept drawing her even after I heard my mother say to my father, "She is still drawing those witches, Bob. Should we be concerned? They are *witches.*" "Only if we find out she can do magic," I heard my father reply in a voice that was not preoccupied, not concerned. I hid behind the kitchen door and listened. I could always find ways to listen in and that seemed a step in the magical direction.

III.

I didn't know how to revise the final part about my older brother and his friends playing pool in the game room one June day near the end of third grade. They were going to graduate. Some had something call draft papers. My brother said he got his, too. I enjoyed their fun, the nick names they had for each other, Monkey, ToJo, STP. I didn't have to hide around them. They didn't care what I heard. And sometimes they lifted me so I could shoot at the white cue ball toward any ball they thought I could get into a pocket. They let me cue up their sticks. Monkey said he knew a guy already who was in Vietnam and his sister said his letters home were all about cool things he was doing. My oldest brother and the others with these papers all gave hand slaps until my mother walked into the game room.

My mother was beautiful walking into that room.
It must have been close to the time my father got home because her hair was curled and her lipstick was on. She was always the most beautiful when she was waiting for my father. She told me to scat and ordered the boys to follow her to the kitchen. I dragged upstairs to my room but then stealthed right back down

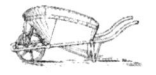

and found a perfect hiding spot under the dining room buffet. My mother said, "If you want to see cool things that you will be doing in Vietnam, look at this." She reached for a magazine on the top of the Frigidaire. The magazine was passed from boy to boy, none of them hand slapping now. None of them even speaking. I heard STP speak first. "Sorry, Mrs. Nightengale." I heard my brother say he was sorry, too. And then the magazine was put back out of reach and I heard my mother tell them not to let the little kids get their hands on it. But I did. When the coast was clear I drew chair to counter and stood on the counter at eye view of the top of that pee green Frigidaire. It was a <u>Life</u> magazine. The folded down pages showed naked girls running. I think they were on fire. I think they were my age. That lifesaver feeling crawled back into my belly. I got down without noise and joined everyone in the living room watching Wild Kingdom. I passed on the popcorn.

IV.

My oldest brother worked a few days after school at the milk bottling plant. One night during dinner, a few days after I sneaked to the top of the refrigerator, the phone rang. It was for my Dad. My brother had been hurt. "How hurt?" dad said. He repeated the answer and the rest of the conversation back to my mother as if the rest of us were not at the table. *"He has cut off his finger. His trigger finger. That's it then. He's not going. The supervisor says it is a mystery. The safety guards had been checked. They were all up. This shouldn't have happened. The guard rails were checked and up."* I managed a scoop of corn thinking the "Fractured Fairy Tale" witch that I drew on that <u>Life</u> magazine to protect the running girls, to help them find their mothers, may have played some magic for my brother, too.

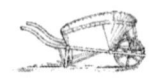

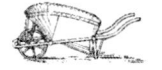

Season of Decay

It was the season of decay
for tulips when he got the call.
Petals brown, fallen, lost in the green
of newness yet coming, but for one tulip
smaller than the others and bright
with a color of gold and peach blend.
She stood silent and straight even
in wind as if guarding the fallen
yellow men among her. It takes time
for tulips to decay. They must mulch
down before they are cut down,
all gardeners know this: There will be
no blooms next year
if you pull and cut the rot too early.

The uncle had decayed west
of this garden where he waited years
to mold to mulch.
A single tulip fallen alone
among magazines and television guides,

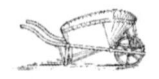

among stones of red and orange

and a single golden rock.

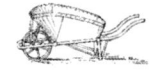

Winter's Valentine

The February window opens
my heart like a stent: a wandering
swirl of frost flakes in shapes of capillaries
cover the edges of larger arteries in shapes that
call me to feel, remember, *know*
the warmth of my own heartbeat.
Through the window's bluish veins
I see ice crystal valentines swinging
in the tender limbs among the chill around
the weeping cherry tree.

And then the sun.

The sun pierces its lit arrow, and the crystal hearts
begin to drip rainbow drops of blood:
Winter sending a love note to stir my heart, melt my heart,
burst my heart, break my heart, mend my heart?
I watch as water now trickles predictably, playfully
giving life which *is* love after all
to the winter hardened earth, and with each
melting, water filled sugar candy kiss to the solid ground,
winter birds are crying and singing at the same time,
just as my heart does,
as cupid plays in the warming cold
among the tree limbs, along my window edges.

Weeping and Laughing

It is morning and
the weeping cherry tree
is in hysterics
laughing pink petals of joy.

My coffee cup steams
a facial wash over my
fallen face and I cry and
laugh at the same time

having just learned
that a tree, a gathering
of petals and coffee steam
are what I have been waiting
for all my life.
Right there.

The Night Aunt Goldie Died

an early snow brought a path of white
and black zebra tracks to the ground a thousand miles away
from her breathing.
The tracks, the snow, the early air
carried a sigh. *A Sigh.*

Autumn plants left uncut, bloomed again with white clusters
that couldn't be cut, brought in, smelled into recognition.
Instead, they stood as a clump of messengers
carrying that sigh on a night
as cold as the salmon she would have shipped,
cold as a man alone with coldness only a boyhood could recall
one thousand miles away from the zebra's coat of snow,
As the sigh,
oh that sigh,
was heard clearly as news calling
from the other side of those thousand miles.

The flight of the sigh, *oh this last sigh,*
moved through the desert,
over mountains, under rivers, past cities
where a woman, a girl really, with dreams of snow as zebra hide,
sat alone on back steps,
caught the sigh,
held the sigh,
savored it like a last breath,
and slumping her saddened shoulders,
blew back the single, cold curl of the sigh,
blew it back to the desert, blew it back to the man.

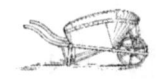

When the Creaking Started

A tree in the yard beyond mine
is dying. It stands taller than the
highest homes in this old neighborhood.
Its branches all but barren,
the thin stretches of the
highest and smallest limbs
leave dark cobwebs in the sky.
A blackbird perches amidst the
death and the tree trembles
with the weightlessness of winged life.

An old man walks under the tree,
his hands gnarled around a cane
the same coffee with cream color
of the branches which have gone
naked with the loss of black bark.
Children skate board smoothly past the man.
They take and need no shade,
their limbs light, swinging in rhythm.
They do not look up at the old man
or dying tree-- each bending into trembles.

I hear the creaking in my neck
as I turn from these children to
an old man and back to a dying tree.

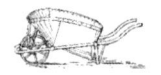

Things Left Behind

Mrs. Kowalski comes to my door with cookies
the size of a dessert plate. I put on the tea kettle
my mother left behind for me. My neighbor, 86,
tells me again about the Heslinskis who built my house.
My deed says built in 1913. The coal pile in my basement
came with the house; the clean and haul away company
of men with arms like shovels couldn't carry the coal away.
Told me to "keep it lady, save yourself the charge."

If my furnace goes, due any time now, I figure I have
the coal and could break a city ordinance with a fire
to warm the deficit bottom of my feet, hands, savings account.
We keep the coal pile a secret, but we talk about the fences. The
neighborhood is fenced now; over the cookies and tea she tells me
that before the fences,
before and between the wars,
they shared their lawns for gardens. I listened, indebted.

"One grew corn, cucumbers, another tomatoes, another squash,
another beans and berries and then we harvested, sorted, shucked,
shared and canned in Mrs. Walaski's kitchen; she had an extra
canning kitchen," she says, "and we would divide the Ball jars
and stock our basement shelves for winter."

"A man came by last winter and bought all my Ball jars
for three cents each," she says between bites.
"My daughter said I got taken. Scolded me and said any jar with
Ball on it is worth something now." I do not tell her how I keep
pennies now in a Ball jar I found in my basement.

"But the shared soil is gone now like my friends, she says,
dead or left behind for Florida." I think of gardens receded.

"I keep rubber bands though, and clean bits of tin foil and wax
paper and cooking oil in a can by the sink," Mrs. Kowalski tells.
"Some weeks, she says, I have no trash bag to put out for the city

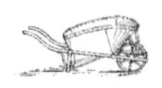

truck, but when my daughter visits there're two on the curb and the boys on the truck yell out, 'Your kid's here for a visit Mrs. Kowalski?'

"Oh, and the lights. Don't get me started on the lights," she says. "Don't get me started on the lights people leave on when they leave rooms behind."

I bite into a cookie and think of my pile of coal left behind.

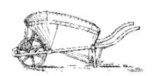

Sunflowers At Highway Speed

A bend in the highway blocked the view
as traffic ahead slowed, noticeably slowed.
An accident for sure to delay the line of
cars moving to the next place on the day's lists.

But the bend straightened with no bent car in crash, instead

a field of sunflowers stretching their long
green legs and bowing their gold and bronze tiaras
waving to us in the wind

as we slowed in synchronicity, necks turned
all in a slow row, all without word called ahead
one car to the other;

all in awe of a quarter mile stretch of a sunflower field
we slowed our wasteful to dos and foul fuel
to abandon hurry and know for a few slow moments
the green and yellow stretch we forgot to write on lists.

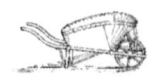

Looking for My Mother

Takes me to Maple Grove Cemetery
but after moments of ministration,
I take the muddy road out
through the gate, and something

Takes me to Elizabeth's house on Kingston Road
instead where a collection of tea cups are a
careful composition and books stare in stately stacks
 in a room of etchings where penciled scratches
on a crossword wait on the sofa, where she has
filled six blanks across on the *New York Times*
puzzle for the week for six letters for: 'word for looks after.'

Takes me to my closet where a green coat
hangs because Elizabeth said, "It's your color."

Takes my eyes to the ring of emerald
on my finger given me by my father
many years after it was given
first to my mother.

Takes me to my garden where white tulips,
once bulbs pulled from clumps in the Kingston Road
soil "would do better, " Elizabeth says, "in your
loam." They will die off too. I know. But later.
Their quicker take of leave will
make room for pink phlox, another gift
from the gardens on Kingston Road,
but now these white tulips tug at deep dirt
rototilled round my heart:

Takes me to that crossword puzzle again
where six letters *could* spell: friend, tender,
mother.

The Daughter of a Tenant Farmer's Son

Learned that shoes are important.
Saving pennies to buy saddle shoes
for her, her sisters, buster brown
for the brothers

To tap away at his friend's French Canadian
voice and rhythm guitar
singing wanting songs of Roger Miller

And the green low garden shoes
which snugged the feet and the loam
as she learned from him the difference
from a green bean's first budding and the
weeds that interrupted the warm earth

Shoes not made of felt from the government
but from work in fingers poking seeds
into earth, made of food for winter
shoes so warm they glowed like coal
in the black stove

Feet wrapped in sandwich bags
to provide the gay glide into a woman

who could buy the clicking soles
of memory from farm soil
to the glistening floors of freedom
found on waxed surfaces of a college
hoping to teach students that
how we get shoes is important.

Tillable Soil

You must wait for spring.
You must wait for the earth
To be dry, warm.
You must push your fingers
Into the ground and dare the dirt
To ball up in your hands;
If the ball crumbles
You begin.

You cannot rush tilling soil.
This is precise work.
It is work that must make your
heart pound as if your lover's face
has suddenly appeared behind
you as you smooth your hair in the mirror
of pooled water.

Tilling is the sweaty work
of striking a hoe row by row.
Tilling is precise work.
As hands and feet tremble
with the work, you mark
a place for peonies, petunias, primrose.

You know that rains will come,
seeds will sprout with memory
of last year's mother plant.
You know that you and this work
will leave one day as autumn turns to draft.
You will end the tilling.
As you stoop, you hear the soil call:

We will sing in rains, we will keep your salty taste
after you are gone. We will cover you.
We will cry for your slender slide against

the greenest stalks. We will sway in the songs
of your humming voice among the beds
where you cast out snails with beer,
placed rocks from the sea to support
our fallen folly on rain soaked and dry days.
We will push through this tilled soil
startled by machine cranked lines
to wait like a humbled child
chasing the fragrance left behind
when you worked our loam to tillable.

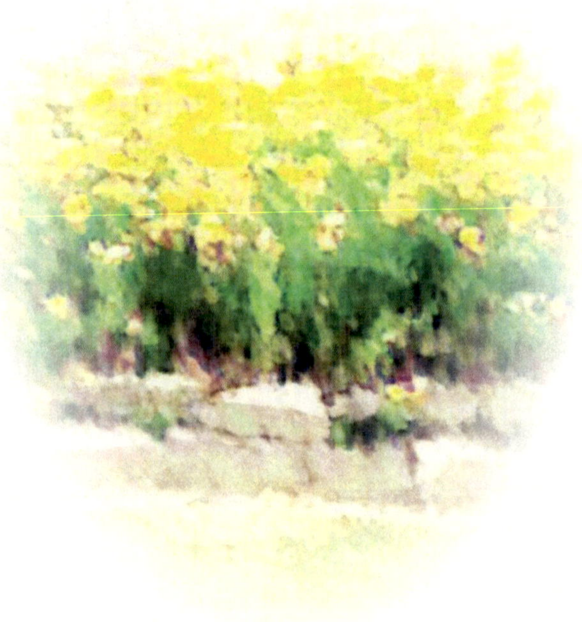